30 Days
To Stop
Obsessing

A Mindfulness Program with a Touch of Humor

Harper Daniels

Copyright © PJV 2019

This book is meant to be a guide only, and does not guarantee specific results. If the lessons and exercises in this book are followed, change can occur for certain people. Results vary from person to person; some people may not need to complete the thirty days to experience change, but it's encouraged that the entire program be read completely through at least once.

The last half of the book consists of note pages that the reader can use in conjunction with the exercises for each day. The reader is encouraged to utilize the note pages; though it's not necessary.

Check out more mindfulness guides at:

www.30DaysNow.com

Contents

Preface……………………………………………………4

Day 1……………………………………………………...7
Day 2………………………………………………………8
Day 3………………………………………………………9
Day 4……………………………………………………..10
Day 5……………………………………………………..11
Day 6……………………………………………………..12
Day 7……………………………………………………..13
Day 8……………………………………………………..14
Day 9……………………………………………………..15
Day 10……………………………………………………16
Day 11……………………………………………………17
Day 12……………………………………………………18
Day 13……………………………………………………19
Day 14……………………………………………………20
Day 15……………………………………………………21
Day 16……………………………………………………22
Day 17……………………………………………………23
Day 18……………………………………………………24
Day 19……………………………………………………25
Day 20……………………………………………………26
Day 21……………………………………………………27
Day 22……………………………………………………28
Day 23……………………………………………………29
Day 24……………………………………………………30
Day 25……………………………………………………31
Day 26……………………………………………………32
Day 27……………………………………………………33
Day 28……………………………………………………34
Day 29……………………………………………………35
Day 30……………………………………………………36

Conclusion……………………………………………….37
Note Pages……………………………………Begins on 38

Preface

Obsession is oftentimes misunderstood as passion. Whereas *passion* is a deep and positive affection derived from our natural devotion to something; *obsession* is a self-generated and devitalizing desire that grows stronger as it's self-imposed upon one's own experience. In other words, you conceive and maintain your obsessions in a cycle of self-inflicting compulsion. If you have ever been in the grips of obsession, then you know how debilitating it can be. This mindfulness program will help you to stop the chaotic cycle of obsession, so that you can live your best life possible in the present moment.

For the purpose of this book, let's define *obsession* as: an attachment to the misconception that you can secure an experience, thing, or person for obtaining happiness. It can even be described as a strong desire to attain and exploit an experience, thing, or person for your own satisfaction. If these definitions appear too complex, feel free to define *obsession* any way you wish, as long as you recognize it as an adverse attachment to a misperception of happiness.

The following pages involve a 30 day mindfulness program made up of lessons and exercises to help you overcome patterns of thinking, feelings, and attachments that have kept you stuck in a state of obsession. Though these lessons and exercises can be applied to any unhealthy reliance, this program will focus specifically on the experience of the obsessive state.

For some readers, they'll overcome the old reliance quickly and will drop the unhealthy thoughts and dependency in no time; and for others, they'll overcome the attachment slowly and gradually. In either case, if you stick with the program, you'll start to witness yourself obsessing less.

Please don't judge your progress in the program, as this isn't a competition and there isn't a goal you must attain. Let the old thoughts, feelings, habits, and attachment simply drop as you work through the exercises and lessons.

It's not necessary to complete the program's days in order, nor should you be religious about completing them successfully. There is no such thing as a successful completion of this program. The bottom line is to observe and awaken, and that cannot be obtained through success, force, pressure, struggle, or competition. Simply relax, follow the program, and you'll begin to stop obsessing.

You'll also notice that mindfulness, silence, and stillness are a regular discipline for each day in the program. Because you've been influenced by a dependency based society that demands instant gratification, silence and stillness may seem nearly impossible for you to practice. For this reason, we'll incorporate this discipline from the outset. A quiet and still mind is an incredibly powerful resource, but one that requires daily maintenance. It should also be noted that you're not required to fight the feelings that accompany obsession; however, if you've already dropped the attachment, then do not pick it up again. The point being: by practicing the following exercises and lessons in the days to come, you won't even need willpower to stop obsessing – it'll just happen.

You'll need about 15-30 minutes per day for the program; but feel free to spend more time if needed. The amount of time doesn't matter, as long as you're in an environment that allows you to concentrate without distraction. Also to be mentioned, the last 30 pages of this book are clear note pages that correspond to the 30 days. It's encouraged that you write down any thoughts, insights, adaptations, lessons, mantras, etc, on those blank pages. The note pages can also be used to rip out and take with you. Feel free to use them as you wish.

One last thing: If you're like most people, you might be dependent on caffeine, alcohol, or sugar to some extent. If you are, do your best to lessen the consumption of these substances over the next 30 days. It's not necessary that you abstain, but can you cut consumption of these substances in half, or more? It's important that your mind is sober and your body relaxed to make the most of these exercises and lessons.

Let's get started.

Day 1

Exercise:

Find a place without distraction, and turn off all electronics. Sit with your back straight, kneel, or lie on a hard surface (not bed) and remain in silence for 10 minutes.

During these 10 minutes, take deep and focused breaths and hold them for a few seconds each. Exhale slowly. Listen intently to your breathing. Don't try to change it – simply listen, and feel the air go in and out.

*When you're ready, repeat the mantra: "**Be still. Be silent.**" Repeat this slowly multiple times out loud as well as quietly. You might experience boredom or anxiety, but continue repeating the mantra regardless. Repeat it until you're calm and focused. You can continue the deep breathing during the mantra, or take deep breaths during pauses. Don't rush.*

Each of the 30 days will have this time of silence, focused breathing, and a mantra. Except for this page, the end of each day will remind you of the minutes you are to spend in silence and focused breathing; and will also have a mantra for you to practice. You can repeat the mantras during your times of silence and focused breathing, or following. Remember, there is no right or wrong way to do this.

Adverse thoughts and feelings want to fight; in fact, they're energized by fighting. Instead of fighting obsession, meet it with silence and observation. Let the exercises and lessons in this program guide you.

Day 2

Exercise:

Ponder this question: Can you remember a point in your life when you did not experience obsession?

Writing is extremely beneficial to the mind; especially when pondering. Write down your thoughts about this particular question. If your mind drifts, then write whatever thoughts emerge. It's okay if you have nothing to write, but ponder the question regardless.

Were you able to remember a period in your life when you weren't experiencing obsession? If you're like many people, you may have to return to memories of childhood to determine that period. It's not uncommon for a person to experience obsession early on, and continue experiencing it throughout life. We're encouraged early, in school and family, to obsess about specific societal desires; and as a result, an attachment to obsession is born. Many people are taught to feel obsessed about particular experiences that are thought to lead to happiness; however, happiness can never be attained through obsession, and it's not necessary to keep an attachment to an obsessive state of being.

Recognize that obsession is a learned misperception with roots. However, it can be dropped quickly and completely; and you have the capability to drop it. In other words, you are not controlled, identified, or dominated by a learned misconception of happiness. It's an adverse illusion that you no longer have to live with; it's time to leave it be. Obsession is a conditioned response that can be unlearned

*10 minutes of silence and focused breathing. Repeat the mantra: **"Drop. Unlearn. Discover."**

Day 3

Exercise:

Pinch the skin on the back of your hand or forearm until there is discomfort and slight pain. It's not necessary to pinch hard enough to bruise yourself, just enough to feel a small burn.

Did I cause the pain by asking you to do this exercise? No; you caused this pain to yourself – think about this carefully. You even decided how much pain to give yourself, and when to relieve the pain. You can't blame me or anyone else for the pain you just experienced. You were solely responsible. You were also responsible for letting go.

This is easily understood with regard to physical pain, such as pinching oneself; however, we have a lot of difficulty understanding this lesson as it applies to adverse emotions and feelings, such as obsession.

How often have you said, and have heard others say, *"He makes me so angry when…"*, *"I'm depressed because she…"*, or *"I'm so frustrated that they…"* No person ever makes you experience obsession or negative feelings. It's always you who are causing them; and then placing the blame on others. Essentially, you are emotionally pinching yourself and not letting go. People go their entire lives without releasing the pinch. Instead of letting go, they scream at others, *"Release the pain! Let go! Fix this! Stop this! You're to blame!"* Wake up and see that you are solely responsible for letting go of the pain, and you can do it now.

*10 minutes of silence and focused breathing. Repeat the mantra: **"I can release negative feelings, here and now."**

Day 4

Exercise:

Count to 25 slowly, pausing for a few seconds before the next number; then, count backward from 25 slowly. Try this with your eyes closed. While counting up you can imagine yourself being lifted into the sky; and then while counting down, descending back to earth.

Our world today is about speed. Everyone seems to be in a rush, yet most of people are unsatisfied; and, they have no clue where they're going. Chasing the next best thing is a fruitless endeavor. It's the rare person who slows down to enjoy the present moment, regardless of its nature. Because there seems to be so many problems, and most jobs are focused on resolving those problems, people are compelled to obsess and rush toward a reward and conclusion. That surely isn't happiness. Happiness can only be found in the present moment, not in a hypothetical future of rewards and successes. Rushing is another form of going nowhere.

How many times have you rushed through thinking and problem solving? This is destructive to your peace of mind and health: concentration suffers, stress levels rise, and awareness to the present moment isn't possible.

It's critical to slow down. You only have one life to live – don't rush through it obsessively, and don't be dependent on anything that encourages you to rush and obsess. Be still, and slow down.

*10 minutes of silence and focused breathing. Repeat the mantra: "**Slow down. Do not rush. Enjoy the present moment.**"

Day 5

Exercise:

Observe your body. Observe how it feels, moves, and reacts. More direction is explained below.

If you're experiencing obsession today, observe your body movements, sounds, sensations, and breaths during the experience. Do your eyes widen? How do you breathe? Do you move fast or slow? What's the tone of your voice? How is your posture? Do you sweat? Try to observe everything about your body while you're obsessing. Be aware of obsession's affect on your body.

If you are not experiencing obsession today, then continue with the 10 minutes of silence and focused breathing, but get in touch with your body. A good way to do this is by touching each body part and saying its name, leaving your hand on the part for a few seconds and feeling its texture and warmth. Start with your head: place your hand on your head and say, "*I am touching my head.*" And then work your way down to your shoulders, arms, stomach, legs, knees, and feet. Focus your attention on one body part at a time. Say its name and describe what you are touching. Go as slow as you can; don't rush the observation.

Like many adverse attachments, obsession can trick you into believing that it's in control of your body; and it can go so far as to make you believe that you're its puppet. Take your body back by becoming aware through observation. Mindfully observing your body when you're feeling anxious is a wonderful way to expose the lie of obsession.

*10 minutes of silence and focused breathing. Repeat the mantra: "**I am not my body.**"

Day 6

Exercise:

Clean something slowly. Take your time; don't rush the cleaning, and be thorough. You can clean your room, car, kitchen, bathroom, bag, desk drawer, shoes…anything. Go slow, and give full attention to what you're doing. Throw away as much stuff as possible.

Most of us hate cleaning and only do it when the mess has become awful; however, cleaning has been known to be a great therapeutic exercise because we attach to our clutter. Regular cleaning is a wonderful practice because we're letting go of disorder in the present moment, in a very practical way.

Similar to a messy kitchen that can look disastrous; the mind can experience obsession because of negative thought clutter. Remember; obsession is an attachment to chaotic thoughts involving false happiness, so the person who's often obsessed is filling the mind and body with stresses that block authentic perception in the present moment. The only way to clear this type of mental clutter is through focused observation, understanding, and awareness.

The exercises in this book are purposed to help clear your mind from the tumultuous mess that obsession leaves, so that you can perceive clearly. If you haven't experienced it already, waking up to a life without obsession is refreshing and exciting.

*10 minutes of silence and focused breathing. Repeat the mantra: *"I am clean. My mind is clear."*

Day 7

Exercise:

Most food products have a "Nutritious Facts" label that will tell you the percentage of fat, cholesterol, sodium, carbohydrates, protein, and other important nutritious content in the product. Let's make one for your experience.

On a sheet of paper, write down the words: happiness, stress, anxiety, worry, anger, and depression. Feel free to add other words that describe emotions and feelings that you may regularly experience. Now, next to each word write down the percentages that best represent their measure in your life. There is no right or wrong for this exercise; the point is to become keenly aware of what emotions and feelings you are experiencing more often than others. If you write 70% depression, that is not "bad." Simply be honest with the percentages; recognize them.

Which emotions received the highest percentages? Which received the lowest? Remember, you are not your emotions or feelings; however, you do experience emotions and feelings, and some of them will be experienced more than others. If you are experiencing adverse emotions more often than positive ones, then don't let that bother you. Whatever emotion you experience in the present moment, observe it and let it pass. For the negative emotions that come regularly, examine them and let them fade. Observe the emotions that arise from an obsessive state of being. Observation is the key to understanding.

*10 minutes of silence and focused breathing. Repeat the mantra: **"I am not ruled by emotion. I am here and now."**

Day 8

Exercise:

Choose a song to listen to carefully. You can choose the song from your music collection; or simply turn on the radio and wait for a song to play.

While listening to the song, don't listen to the notes, beats, voice, or rhythm; instead, listen for the silence between sounds. Listen for the stops, pauses, and absence of sound between notes. Listen for the silence in the song.

Have you ever realized that your favorite songs would not exist without silence? Every note, rhythm, beat, and voice needs a moment of silence to manifest – even if that moment exists in a millisecond. Without silence, there would be no noise, yet alone music. This isn't to say that noise and silence are in conflict; quite the opposite actually. Sounds and silence are complementary. So, were you able to hear the silence within the song? Practice this repeatedly whenever you listen to music. Listen for the silence that allows the music to endure.

Similarly, we need silence to let the rhythm of life manifest. Unfortunately, this has become a struggle for many people, because we live in an unbalanced world that encourages sound over silence. Don't follow noise dependent crowds, and don't fear silence. Silence is a powerful remedy. Practice remaining in silence daily; you'll start to hear and see new and wonderful things. Obsession dissolves in the midst of silence.

*10 minutes of silence and focused breathing. Repeat the mantra: **"Be silent. Listen. Be silent."**

Day 9

Exercise:

Say the words "Guilt", "Shame", and "Regret" 10 times to yourself out loud. Don't rush. Pause between each repetition. For the pause, you can take a deep breath. Your eyes can remain open or closed. Again, don't rush - say the words slowly and observe any thoughts, feelings, or images that emerge internally.

Now, say these words again 10 times, but with a smile.

What futile credence we give words such as Guilt, Shame and Regret. We use these words on ourselves as well as others; they become regular vocabulary for our internal recurring voices. And in the end, they're mere words that hold no power. What would these words be without a facial expression, tone, inflection, or emphasis?

When you said these three specific words, what thoughts came to mind, what did you feel, and was there a reaction in your body? If there is a reaction, such as shortness of breath or a frown, people tend to interrupt it as sadness; but this reaction is a learned behavior. We've been taught to feel and think a certain way with regard to guilt, shame, and regret. The truth is: these words mean nothing.

Obsession, like most dependent states, flourishes on these three words and the learned reactions they produce. But see them for what they are…mere words with no power.

*10 minutes of silence and focused breathing. Repeat the mantra: **"I am not Guilt. I am not Shame. I am not Regret."**

Day 10

Exercise:

Find an object that you can break: an egg, a drinking glass, a pencil...anything. In a safe place, break the object of your choice, and be especially careful if it's glass or something sharp.

Don't clean up the pieces immediately, observe the mess and let the pieces sit for at least a few minutes.

Did you break the object, or did I break the object by directing you to break it? And if you believe it was only you who broke the object, did the object allow you to break it? This isn't an exercise meant to release frustration or stress. The purpose of this lesson is to show you that you're not 100% responsible for your perceived chaos, mess, loss, or broken pieces.

Destruction happens in the present moment, and that's OK. We spend so much time obsessing about goals, plans, relationships, jobs, situations, the future, and other things breaking into pieces. And when that happens, we tend to blame ourselves or others, because that's what we've been taught to do. Allow breaking to happen; and observe the pieces as well as your reaction to the destruction.

*10 minutes of silence and focused breathing. Repeat the mantra: "**I cannot harm or break the present moment.**"

Day 11

Exercise:

Imagine this scenario: Its 3:00 AM. You wake up and realize that your home is on fire. Everyone, except you, is out of the house. You realize that you only have a minute or less to get yourself out before everything is destroyed. You must act immediately.

With such a short amount of time, what do you grab to take with you?

Really consider this scenario; because it happens to people every day around the world. People are forced to leave their homes because of fire, flood, violence, and other uncontrollable factors. If this happened to you, what physical things would you grab and take in such a short window of time? Your cell phone, family pictures, computer, passport, specific files, a project, money, or nothing at all? Whatever you take within that moment will be the most meaningful objects to you. What does this tell you about your anxieties, desires, attachments, concerns, needs, and habits?

If you're ever obsessed about losing or obtaining a material possession, then remind yourself that physical materials are fleeting objects. Never allow obsession to convince you that material possessions are important.

*10 minutes of silence and focused breathing. Repeat the mantra: "**I am not my possessions. I am free from material things.**"

Day 12

Exercise:

Today, look for the color blue in your surrounding environment. If possible, spend the entire day looking for the color blue in the places you go. Whether you're doing this exercise in a bedroom, office, classroom, outside, or while traveling, look for the color blue in all things that surround you. If you think you'll forget to do this throughout the entire day, spend at least 20 focused minutes practicing this exercise at some point.

Focused attention is something that must be practiced - it doesn't come easy in our rapid paced society. Instead of encouraging us to focus and observe, the modern world encourages us to rush and get things done.

Searching for a color or shape helps to slow down our accelerated and cyclical thought patterns, and reminds us that there's more to the world than the chaotic thoughts we collectively and daily experience. By searching for the color blue, your mind can escape the fictitious grip of anxiety, lust, desire, depression, worry, fear, or any other potent emotional attachment. When you're experiencing obsessive thoughts, are you aware of the stunning colors around you? Most likely not.

The obsessive state functions to distract your conscience from present reality. Look for the color blue today, and wake up to life in the present moment.

*10 minutes of silence and focused breathing. Repeat the mantra: "*I am focused, here and now.*"

Day 13

Exercise:

Choose an object that you use and rely on every day, and that you sometimes lose – such as a key, cell phone, pen, hat, toothbrush, or television controller.

Now, actually attempt to lose this object. Hide it well, and try to make yourself forget where it is.

More than likely you won't be able to lose this object, as hard as you try, because you have applied a lot of attention to the process of losing it and trying to make yourself forget. At this point, losing it is nearly impossible. Why do you think this is?

If you try to drop a dependency, behavior, thought pattern, addiction, or any unhealthy vice using a lot of thought, attention, focus, struggle, and effort…you'll never lose it. It will be with you in one form or another for a very long time, possibly forever. The point is: whatever you give attention to consistently, will be difficult to lose. This is the reason why people who complain a lot are never happy – they can't stop giving thought and attention to the problems they're grumbling about. The problems eventually become an intimate part of their lives. Remember, rival enemies maintain a devoted relationship.

The obsessive state of being masterfully influences you to give attention to meaningless and fleeting things. Don't accept the influence; let the obsession be lost.

*10 minutes of silence and focused breathing. Repeat the mantra: **"I do not need to hold on. I allow it to be lost."**

Day 14

Exercise:

On a piece of paper (any size) write down the goals that you've been striving to achieve – i.e. the goals that you believe will bring you fulfillment. For example: a new job, a house in a nice neighborhood, traveling the world, a business, a family, new friends, a degree or certification, building a network, reaching a net worth of a million dollars, etc.

Now, tear up the paper into multiple pieces and throw away.

Goals can be very helpful and useful if they're not obsessed over. However, in the modern world people develop a reliance on goals. Think about all the times you've said something like, *"I need to get that," "I must reach this," "I'll do anything to accomplish that"*, etc. It's often the case that people spend more time worrying about their goals, than freely doing something in the present moment to reach them. Plus, the goal in itself is fleeting, while the journey in the present moment is real and lasting.

The habit of thinking that goals must be met, or else failure ensues, is subtly fixed to dependencies. When you've been obsessed in the past with regard to a goal, what was the goal that you obsessed over? What was it that you felt you needed to achieve?

*10 minutes of silence and focused breathing. Repeat the mantra: **"My happiness does not depend on meeting a goal. I'm happy now."**

Day 15

Exercise:

Using objects that can stack (rocks, books, boxes, containers, pillows, etc), stack them slowly and carefully until they fall.

When the stack collapses, smile and laugh.

The lives of many people are spent stacking things for the goal of success, as defined by society. People stack possessions, knowledge, relationships, degrees, money, jobs, toys, businesses, experiences, etc. They stress, fight, fatigue, compete, become ill, and get anxious and depressed through the process of stacking; yet, few people have found happiness. Society tells us that if our stack is high and mighty, we'll have obtained success. What a deception. What are you stacking; or what do you feel compelled to stack? How is your obsessive state supporting that stack?

Allow the stack to fall. This lesson is not encouraging complacency; but instead teaches that real, authentic, and fulfilling work and action can only happen apart from the stress and worry of stacking. When you stack, you're focused on the future and the perceived importance of the stack; and then you have to maintain that heap of nonsense, which requires a lot of anxiety and pressure. Focus on your experience in the present moment; and if the stack falls, then smile and laugh.

*15 minutes of silence and focused breathing. Repeat the mantra: *"I allow the stack to fall."*

Day 16

Exercise:

Lay down on the floor (not on a bed or couch), with your back straight and your arms at your side. Close your eyes.

Now, imagine yourself in a coffin or under the ground. If this depresses you, do it regardless. With your eyes closed, imagine not being able to open them ever again; also imagine not being able to move your body or speaking ever again. Stay in this position for 10 minutes, or as long as you can.

If this seems gothic or dark, that's only your learned perception of the death experience. There's an ancient teaching that says the way to enlightenment is through a keen awareness of death. The person who is daily reminded that the body will die, and faces this fact head on with a clear mind and acceptance, has nothing to lose and is truly free to live in the present moment. The question isn't whether or not your body will die (because it surely will); the more important question is: will you live before death?

Will you truly live before your body dies? The present moment is the only thing you'll always experience. Instead of fearing a pending death, accept it and be thankful for the present moment; and live in it, without obsessing!

*15 minutes of silence and focused breathing. Repeat the mantra: **"My body will age and pass, but I will always be present."**

Day 17

Exercise:

Find a coin. While standing, flip the coin and let it land wherever. If it lands with the head side up, spin around to the right until you come back to your original place; if it lands tail side up, spin around to the left until you come back to your original place. Again, head side up, spin to the right; tail side up, spin to the left – doing a full circle until you return to your original standing position.

In which direction did you spin? In this exercise you left the direction of your movement completely up to the flip, the coin, and gravity. When you spun, you experienced a specific visual perception of the environment that you would not have had from spinning in the opposite direction. But, you returned to the original position regardless, full circle.

The experience would have been different if you spun to the opposite side; and if you repeat this exercise multiple times, your experiences in the same direction will be different as well. The point being: it doesn't matter what direction you go in or what you experience; you'll always return to the present moment; so the time to be awake, aware, and obsession-free is always…now.

*15 minutes of silence and focused breathing. Repeat the mantra: **"The direction does not matter. I am always here and now, in the present moment."**

Day 18

Exercise:

This exercise may seem frivolous, but give it a try; because it may be one of the lessons that benefit you most.

For the remainder of the day, whenever you use the bathroom, for any reason, take your time with what you're doing. Don't rush through the process, like you may normally do. Focus on taking your time in the bathroom; do every step of your bathroom experience twice as slow. It may even help to say each step: "I am now sitting up straight on the toilet," "I am now putting soap on my hands," "I am now drying my hands," etc.

Most people hurry up their bathroom experience, not realizing what they're doing – forcing, not standing or sitting straight, not relaxing, not washing their hands properly, not drying their hands slowly. They rush in and out, like they have somewhere important to go. Don't be like that any longer. Take your time in the bathroom; it's not only unhealthy for the body to rush the excretion process, but it's also unhealthy for the mind. A rushed bathroom experience doesn't allow you to live in the present moment. Allow the excretion and cleaning to happen naturally with relaxed and focused attention.

One of the goals of obsession is to get you to rush through everything: thoughts, emotions, responses, movements, relationships, and even hygiene. Don't accept the idea that rushing is necessary; it's not necessary, and it's not healthy. Take care of yourself by slowing down.

*15 minutes of silence and focused breathing. Repeat the mantra: **"Don't hurry. Stay present. Stay still."**

Day 19

Exercise:

Think of a major worry that consistently upsets you. On a sheet of paper, write down three worst case scenarios for that dominating concern. For example, if someone is persistently worried about dying alone, that individual can write as a worst case scenario, "I will die alone, without anyone at my side, and without family or loved ones to say goodbye." As mentioned, write down three worst case scenarios for the worry. The worry doesn't have to be as extreme as dying alone; use whichever worry hinders you.

Now, next to each of those three worst case scenarios write, "I accept this." You can either toss the paper or keep it.

Worry is an illness that goes untreated in most people. Think of worry like a cancer of the spirit; but few people know how to treat it effectively. One of the only ways to eradicate worry isn't to fight, ignore, or run from it; but to face it in the present moment and accept it for the illusion it is. You can never be worried about something happening in the present moment – that's impossible. You can only be worried about the future, which is always illusory.

Writing down your worries and worst case scenarios, if they ever do come true (which they rarely do), is a great way to draw those thoughts out of your mind and into the present moment, allowing you to face, accept, and observe them, without obsessing.

*15 minutes of silence and focused breathing. Repeat the mantra: **"Worries are not real. They are passing thoughts."**

Day 20

Exercise:

Spend 5 minutes smelling something aromatic: a piece of fruit, a spice, tea, pine, cedar, a flower, a scented candle, etc. Focus on the smell of that one thing for the entire 5 minutes. Don't let anything distract you from the smell.

How often do you take time to enjoy a fragrant smell? One of the lies of modern society is that if you stop and enjoy your five senses for too long, you'll miss out on…fill in the blank. While people are rushing toward their goals with stress levels spiking, they're totally missing out on awareness in the present moment. People stare at images of food that others have posted on the internet, but don't take the time to slow down and smell or taste real food in the present moment.

What's better: obsessing, or enjoying the smell of vanilla, orange, or pine in the present moment? The first is fake and illusory; the second is real and sensational. Obsession does a great job at stealing time and energy from your other senses, such as smell. One of the best ways get into the present moment and away from an illusion is through focusing on smell and the use of your other senses. Don't let obsession diminish your other senses any longer.

*15 minutes of silence and focused breathing. Repeat the mantra: **"I can sense the present."**

Day 21

Exercise:

Light a candle and observe its flame for 5 minutes. Watch it move and feel its heat. Appreciate its energy.

Now, blow out the flame.

(If you don't have a candle, light a match and blow it out; and if you don't have a candle or match, stare at a dim light for 5 minutes and then turn it off.)

The temperature of a small candle flame (and match flame) is around 1200 Celsius (which is about 2000 Fahrenheit). That's a lot of energy! And within a fraction of a second, it was extinguished as you blew it out; or in the case of the light, turned off its energy source. There wasn't a gradual process with delays and stops. You blew out the highly energized flame, and that was it - from 1200 Celsius to nonexistent in no time; or should I say, in present no time.

We're fooled into believing that our emotional attachments have a lot of energy and power. It's not just obsession, but all adverse attachments survive on this deception of power. The truth is: obsession doesn't have energy like the candle flame, though your mind may have been tricked into believing it does. The candle flame is real and powerful; whereas obsessive thoughts are illusory and fictitious.

As easily and quickly as you extinguished the flame, you can drop obsessive thoughts in the present moment.

*15 minutes of silence and focused breathing. Repeat the mantra: **"Dependency isn't real. It can be extinguished."**

Day 22

Exercise:

Stand still for 5 minutes; with knees slightly bent (i.e. your legs should not be locked). At first try to remain still, but then let your body sway. Let it move any way it wishes. Feel its movement. If you're unable to stand, you can do this same exercise by extending your arm or leg from a sitting position – try to keep it straight, but then let go of trying and allow movement to happen.

We seem to lock ourselves into goals, expectations, thought patterns, and plans. We even go so far as to admire and honor rigidity – people mistake rigidity for perseverance. This is taught and told to us by our culture. Everything around you may be shouting, even in a quiet whisper, that you must remain submissive and obedient.

Obsession, like most toxic conditions, is no different in its message. It wants you to remain rigid; not to be released from its hold. If you freely moved on from the state of obsession, it would lose you as a dependent. By the way, who wants to remain rigidly dependent on something like obsession for their security? Or I should say false security.

The message of obsession essentially says, *"You need me, and I need you. Without me, you would sway to your own rhythm and lose control. I keep you grounded and safe."* Allow your body and mind to move on from this deception. Trust that your body and mind will sway to its own rhythm, and away from the state of obsession.

*15 minutes of silence and focused breathing. Repeat the mantra: "**I am now free to move. I am free to move on.**"

Day 23

Exercise:

Turn off your cell phone, or put it in airplane mode, for at least 1 hour, and observe the thoughts you experience. If you don't have any major responsibilities this day, or if you have all you need and don't require the phone, then turn off your cell phone for 12 hours. This exercise works best if you can go 24 hours without your cell phone activated; but go no less than 1 hour. If there are people who are immediately dependent on you, send them a text saying that you'll be unavailable, and then turn off your phone.

Like never before, we live in a world with a plethora of distractions. All of these distractions fight for our attention, because money is behind the scenes. Every business is wondering how they can break your distraction from one thing so that you can be distracted by their thing – whether that thing is a product or service. It's a constant war for your attention, response, and reaction. Whoever can hold your attention the longest, wins the battle; but whoever can make you dependent, wins the war. Social media has become an important weapon in this war of distraction; and the smartphone is the gateway. It's time to power off.

When you turned off your phone, what thoughts emerged? Were you concerned that you weren't receiving certain messages, missing out on the latest news, skipping great deals, etc? The obsessive state wants you to stay distracted; so do everything you can to diminish outside distractions.

*15 minutes of silence and focused breathing. Repeat the mantra: **"I am not distracted. I am present, here, and now."**

Day 24

Exercise:

On a sheet of paper (one that you can easily save and return to later) make a list of hobbies that you've had in the past but have neglected, and also make a list of hobbies that you would like to start in the future.

From these lists choose one hobby from the past and one new hobby that you'd like to start. Focus only on these two – the old hobby and the new one. Make this a priority.

How often have you said, or have heard other people say, "*I wish I had the time.*" You do have the time. You just choose to think of time in the way that you've been taught to perceive it. If your life depended on it, you would certainly make the time if needed.

In fact, time is a manmade construct - don't ever forget that. There is only the present moment. Past and future are not here and now. We spend far too much time thinking about time. How many of your recurrent inner thoughts involve questions such as, "*When will that ever happen?*" "*When will I ever change?*" "*Why did that have to happen?*" "*If the past were different, life would be better.*" These are lies that only eat into the present moment, and infect our modern world.

The obsessive state of being occupies the present moment; and that moment could be used to pursue hobbies that magnify your happiness.

*15 minutes of silence and focused breathing. Repeat the mantra: "**The time is now. Happiness is present.**"

Day 25

Exercise:

Go for a mindfulness walk for at least 10 minutes. Focus on each step. Feel the steps: the feel of your feet hitting the ground, your heel rolling forward, your toes, the bend of your knees, your hips working to balance your posture, the swinging of your arms, etc. Don't rush; go slow. Focus on your breathing as well. Get in tune with your body. Pay attention to your physical senses throughout the walk. Focus – don't listen to music or be distracted.

Human beings have always used walking as a naturally restorative exercise. There is something about walking, and focusing on the walk, that calms the mind and soul. The longer one walks, the more relaxed one feels.

Any moment is a good time to walk and experience your inner and outer environment. During long walks, thoughts will emerge that will allow you to consciously observe them. Let the thoughts pass; you may even have emotions that emerge, observe those and let them pass as well. Focusing on your steps will help you clear the mind of clutter. Walking in the early morning and at dusk is especially beneficial.

A 20 minute walk brings more comfort, stillness, peace, focus, and awareness than thousands of hours of obsessing. Walk every day, as much as you can.

*15 minutes of silence and focused breathing. Repeat the mantra: "**I am relaxed. I am at peace.**"

Day 26

Exercise:

Hold a smile for 5 minutes. You don't need to do this exercise in front of a mirror; but feel free to do so if you wish. You can even do this exercise during the 15 minutes of silence and focused breathing. While holding your smile, take a moment and feel your face; actually touch the smile and the curvature of your lips and cheek bones.

Have you ever behaved a certain way and then saw your mood change immediately? Physical exercise, such as running and weightlifting, does this for many people. Certain forms of yoga have also been used by people to change their moods. The point is: changing your behavior not only impacts other people, but can also impact your perception of yourself.

You'll notice that while you're smiling during this exercise, you may experience certain emotions. You might feel silly, embarrassed, stupid, funny, weird, or whatever. Continue smiling regardless. In fact, if you are still experiencing obsession at this point in the program, smile while you're obsessing – hold the smile until the obsessive thoughts pass; set a reminder alarm if needed. As always, observe your thoughts while you're smiling; observe the thoughts as if they're clouds passing by in a bright blue sky.

Smiling causes an authentic reaction in our bodies and minds that is essentially good. The present moment enjoys a nice smile. So hold that smile until you no longer can.

*15 minutes of silence and focused breathing. Repeat the mantra: **"Happiness is now. I am happy."**

Day 27

Exercise:

Choose a physical symbol that will remind you to observe and be aware in the present moment. Try to choose something from nature, or that is made of natural material.

The object you choose can be anything, but it's best if it's something that you can enjoy looking at and touching. For example, many walkers and hikers will find a unique rock small enough to carry in their hands. A stone, necklace, bracelet, seashell, cedar block, coin…anything will do, as long as you enjoy it and you can dedicate it as a tool for remembrance.

Another cunning trick of obsession is to confuse the mind into forgetting you're part of the natural world. The obsessive state requires you to use imagination, which can be easily manipulated. Thus, you're taken out of physical reality. By having a symbol of remembrance, you can reconnect with the present moment. This symbol isn't meant to be an idol, god, or icon. Don't think too deeply into this. The symbol is simply a tool to help you remember where you are in the *here and now*. As long as you're aware of the present, you'll have no desire to return to the hallucination of obsessive thought patterns.

*15 minutes of silence and focused breathing. Repeat the mantra: **"All is well. Here and now, all is well."**

Day 28

Exercise:

Stand in front of a doorway, with the door open. Close your eyes, and take a deep breath. With eyes closed and holding your breath, step through the doorway. Once you have stepped through completely, open your eyes and exhale.

Doorways offer great lessons for practicing mindfulness and observation. How often do you rush through doors without paying attention to the change of environment? We don't often pay attention or appreciate the transition; we simply rush through unaware that our perspective has changed. This isn't a bad thing; in fact, it's great that we don't stall in front of doorways, too afraid to enter the next environment. At the beginning of this exercise you were in a particular place, and then you stepped through a doorway into a completely different setting. You made a transition without obsession, worry, or concern, and very naturally.

When it comes to physical doorways, we rarely stop and worry about the change of environment – we just walk through and accept the new experience. You can apply this same lesson to decisions that have you obsessed, stressed, anxious, or worried. Step through the decisions and accept the changes; but try to step through aware and grateful. There will always be new doorways manifested, leading to new experiences.

*15 minutes of silence and focused breathing. Repeat the mantra: **"I accept change with awareness and gratitude."**

Day 29

Exercise:

Make yourself laugh for 5 minutes. Don't stop laughing. You might feel strange, weird, embarrassed, or stupid...it doesn't matter, just laugh. Try to laugh alone and without the aid of a comedy or joke. If you don't know how to start, just start making the noises that typically accompany your laughter.

What feelings did you experience during this exercise? Many people report feeling embarrassed or goofy, which is great; however, most people also report a feeling of relief and buoyancy when they've completed this exercise.

Similar to holding a smile, laughing for 5 minutes is a fantastic way to come into present awareness. If you think about it, humor is necessary for life. How sad is the person who is unable to laugh at the experiences of life? After all, life is funny, even the dreadful and lousy experiences.

If you ever again experience adverse thoughts and feelings that accompany the obsessive state, simply laugh at them. Consider how crazy and frivolous it is to obsess, and your reactions to the obsessive state of being; it really is a funny attachment. No other living thing on the planet is bothered by a misconception of expectations, needs, and happiness. The entire situation is comical. If you perceive obsession for what it truly is - a fictitious, impractical, and frivolous attachment – then it can be easily dropped. You must learn to laugh at it. Genuinely laugh the obsessive state away.

*15 minutes of silence and focused breathing. Repeat the mantra: **"Life is wonderful, funny, and real."**

Day 30

Exercise:

Take a piece of paper (one that you can keep) and write down all that you are grateful for – these things don't have to be in any particular order of importance.

Next to each thing you list, write "Thank you."

The person who isn't thankful for all that life gives is typically quite miserable; and obsession thrives on that negativity. The truly grateful person can let go of anything at anytime. A thankful person is always a happy person, so practice gratitude daily.

Have you ever heard anyone say, *"I'm so grateful for obsession"*? Nobody is thankful for the obsessive state; which is a clear sign that it's an unhealthy attachment. However, a few people have learned to be thankful for the present moment experience, despite obsessing.

Not only is it unhealthy, but an attachment to obsession discourages a grateful mind and soul. With only one life to live in the present moment, it's important to always emphasize a grateful heart. Spend time with people who are grateful, and do things that nourish a thankful heart in the present moment. Anything that encourages the obsessive state isn't worth giving attention to. Be thankful, always.

15 minutes of silence and focused breathing. Repeat the mantra: "I am grateful. I am thankful.**"*

Conclusion

The exercises and lessons in this program taught and encouraged observation, awareness to your present moment experience, change of perception, and awakening to true happiness, which can only be found here and now. You were shown that your negative thoughts and feelings are not caused by obsession, or any unhealthy misperception or attachment, but are solely within you and illusory; which means that you are capable of letting those thoughts and feelings pass and dropping the obsessive state in the present moment.

As mentioned at the beginning, there were no goals or measures of success for this program. If you were hoping to find validation or courage to fight obsession, then you may be spending too much time struggling and thinking about the obsessive state. This was not meant to be a struggle or competition, but a release. You don't need to gain freedom from obsession; you already have it.

Life is not meant to be spent dealing with obsession, or any type of unhealthy misperception. Wake up to the present moment and enjoy your present experience. If you've made it through the program, you are certainly more awakened then when you started; however, don't give up mindfully practicing observation of thoughts and feelings, stillness, silence, deep and focused breathing, allowing everything to pass, laughing, smiling, and being grateful.

Live wonderfully awakened and aware…with or without obsession.

Notes for Day 1

(Use the space below to write down thoughts, reminders, ideas, new mantras, revelations, lessons, modifications to the exercise, experiences, etc.)

Notes for Day 2

(Use the space below to write down thoughts, reminders, ideas, new mantras, revelations, lessons, modifications to the exercise, experiences, etc.)

Notes for Day 3

(Use the space below to write down thoughts, reminders, ideas, new mantras, revelations, lessons, modifications to the exercise, experiences, etc.)

Notes for Day 4

(Use the space below to write down thoughts, reminders, ideas, new mantras, revelations, lessons, modifications to the exercise, experiences, etc.)

Notes for Day 5

(Use the space below to write down thoughts, reminders, ideas, new mantras, revelations, lessons, modifications to the exercise, experiences, etc.)

Notes for Day 6

(Use the space below to write down thoughts, reminders, ideas, new mantras, revelations, lessons, modifications to the exercise, experiences, etc.)

Notes for Day 7

(Use the space below to write down thoughts, reminders, ideas, new mantras, revelations, lessons, modifications to the exercise, experiences, etc.)

Notes for Day 8

(Use the space below to write down thoughts, reminders, ideas, new mantras, revelations, lessons, modifications to the exercise, experiences, etc.)

Notes for Day 9

(Use the space below to write down thoughts, reminders, ideas, new mantras, revelations, lessons, modifications to the exercise, experiences, etc.)

Notes for Day 10

(Use the space below to write down thoughts, reminders, ideas, new mantras, revelations, lessons, modifications to the exercise, experiences, etc.)

Notes for Day 11

(Use the space below to write down thoughts, reminders, ideas, new mantras, revelations, lessons, modifications to the exercise, experiences, etc.)

Notes for Day 12

(Use the space below to write down thoughts, reminders, ideas, new mantras, revelations, lessons, modifications to the exercise, experiences, etc.)

Notes for Day 13

(Use the space below to write down thoughts, reminders, ideas, new mantras, revelations, lessons, modifications to the exercise, experiences, etc.)

Notes for Day 14

(Use the space below to write down thoughts, reminders, ideas, new mantras, revelations, lessons, modifications to the exercise, experiences, etc.)

Notes for Day 15

(Use the space below to write down thoughts, reminders, ideas, new mantras, revelations, lessons, modifications to the exercise, experiences, etc.)

Notes for Day 16

(Use the space below to write down thoughts, reminders, ideas, new mantras, revelations, lessons, modifications to the exercise, experiences, etc.)

Notes for Day 17

(Use the space below to write down thoughts, reminders, ideas, new mantras, revelations, lessons, modifications to the exercise, experiences, etc.)

Notes for Day 18

(Use the space below to write down thoughts, reminders, ideas, new mantras, revelations, lessons, modifications to the exercise, experiences, etc.)

Notes for Day 19

(Use the space below to write down thoughts, reminders, ideas, new mantras, revelations, lessons, modifications to the exercise, experiences, etc.)

Notes for Day 20

(Use the space below to write down thoughts, reminders, ideas, new mantras, revelations, lessons, modifications to the exercise, experiences, etc.)

Notes for Day 21

(Use the space below to write down thoughts, reminders, ideas, new mantras, revelations, lessons, modifications to the exercise, experiences, etc.)

Notes for Day 22

(Use the space below to write down thoughts, reminders, ideas, new mantras, revelations, lessons, modifications to the exercise, experiences, etc.)

Notes for Day 23

(Use the space below to write down thoughts, reminders, ideas, new mantras, revelations, lessons, modifications to the exercise, experiences, etc.)

Notes for Day 24

(Use the space below to write down thoughts, reminders, ideas, new mantras, revelations, lessons, modifications to the exercise, experiences, etc.)

Notes for Day 25

(Use the space below to write down thoughts, reminders, ideas, new mantras, revelations, lessons, modifications to the exercise, experiences, etc.)

Notes for Day 26

(Use the space below to write down thoughts, reminders, ideas, new mantras, revelations, lessons, modifications to the exercise, experiences, etc.)

Notes for Day 27

(Use the space below to write down thoughts, reminders, ideas, new mantras, revelations, lessons, modifications to the exercise, experiences, etc.)

Notes for Day 28

(Use the space below to write down thoughts, reminders, ideas, new mantras, revelations, lessons, modifications to the exercise, experiences, etc.)

Notes for Day 29

(Use the space below to write down thoughts, reminders, ideas, new mantras, revelations, lessons, modifications to the exercise, experiences, etc.)

Notes for Day 30

(Use the space below to write down thoughts, reminders, ideas, new mantras, revelations, lessons, modifications to the exercise, experiences, etc.)

Printed in Great Britain
by Amazon